TOP 10:
The Weirdest
of the Weird

Look for other

titles:

Top 10:
The Weirdest
of the Weird

by Mary Packard

and the Editors of Ripley Entertainment Inc.

illustrations by Ron Zalme

SCHOLASTIC INC.

New York   Toronto   London   Auckland   Sydney
Mexico City   New Delhi   Hong Kong   Buenos Aires

Developed by Nancy Hall, Inc.
Designed by R studio T
Cover design by Atif Toor
Illustration on page 44 by Leanne Franson

ISBN 0-439-72562-3

12 11 10 9 8 7 6 5 4   5 6 7 8 9 10/0

Printed in the U.S.A.
First printing, February 2005

Contents

TOP 10:
The Weirdest
of the Weird

Introduction

The Best of the Best

Welcome to the weird and wonderful world of Ripley's Believe It or Not! During his lifetime, Robert Ripley was a daring adventurer who traveled throughout the world in search of the most bizarre, outrageous, and uncanny facts he could find—all to fill the pages of his newspaper column.

Ripley created his first collection of odd facts in 1918. His early Believe It or Not! cartoons, first published in book form in 1929, was an instant best-seller. Soon after, Robert Ripley signed on as a syndicated cartoonist with King Features, and his column was carried in more than 300 newspapers around the world.

Robert Ripley is no longer with us, but his legacy lives on. Each day more and more amazing stories are added to the already bulging Ripley files. For *Top 10*, the editors of the Believe It or Not! books have sifted through hundreds of thousands of them to create what they believe are the top ten wackiest, weirdest, and most remarkable facts in 15 different categories.

There were so many to choose from, this was no easy task! However, it's safe to say that when it comes to outrageous behavior, for example, two winners would have to be Katzen and Eric Sprague, who did everything in their power to turn themselves into the animals they most admired—a tiger and a lizard! And who could ever forget the self-proclaimed professor of "frogology," Bill Steed, who taught his little croakers how to lift weights? When it comes to animals, it would be hard to top Alex the parrot, who speaks and understands the meaning of more than 100 words. Nor could a little superstar like Twiggy the water-skiing squirrel be overlooked. Of course, no Ripley list of mind-blowing facts would be complete without some creepy pictures. Be prepared to see some shrunken heads, as well as the occasional human skull.

So get ready to read some of the weirdest, wildest, and most outrageous facts ever to appear in one book. See how much you know by taking the Over the Top! quizzes and Ripley's Brain Buster in each chapter. Then go on to the Pop Quiz at the end of the book and figure out your Ripley's rank with the handy scorecard. When you're finished, you're bound to agree with Robert Ripley, who believed that nothing could ever be stranger than the truth.

Believe It!®

Some people go to great lengths to achieve the look they want! Here are our picks for the Top 10 Mad Makeovers!

#10 Omi, Oh My!

An English military officer in World War I, the Great Omi sported tattoos from the top of his head to the bottom of his feet. It took 15 million needle stabs to do the job.

Over the Top!

To reduce the size of her waist, actress Anna Held (1872–1918) . . .

a. wore a steel corset.
b. did 300 sit-ups every day.
c. always held her breath.
d. had her lower ribs surgically removed.

#9 Exaggerated Headlines

During the early 20th century, the Mangbetu people of Central Africa considered elongated heads a sign of beauty and intelligence. To achieve this shape, they bound the heads of infants. In adulthood, both men and women wore hats or wrapped their hair around baskets to make the head look even longer.

#8 Stiff-Necked

Long-necked women are considered beautiful by the Padaung people of Myanmar (formerly Burma). To achieve this look, a female is fitted with a metal necklace in early childhood. More necklace rings are added as she grows until the neck has been stretched to the desired length. The catch? The rings must be worn for life!

#7 On File

In 1974, Renda Long of Glendale, Arizona, started growing her fingernails. By 1985, her longest nail had reached 14.5 inches.

#6 Bearded Wonder

Edwin Smith, a miner during the mid-1800s California gold rush, let his beard grow for 16 years. It reached a length of eight feet—so long that Smith had to hire a servant just to wash and comb it!

#5 That's a Stretch!

In the past, as a means of survival, women of the Sara people of Chad, Africa, tried to make themselves unattractive to slave raiders. In childhood, a girl's lips were pierced and wooden plates inserted. The size of the plates was gradually increased. Eventually, the lower lip was stretched enough that a 14-inch plate could be worn.

#4 Earning Her Stripes

Ever since she was a little girl, Katzen the Catwoman loved cats—but who knew she would try to become one when she grew up! When Katzen turned 18, she had her arms and legs tattooed with tiger stripes. Nine years later, her tattoos were complete, making her the first woman in history to have a full-body theme tattoo, not to mention removable artificial whiskers!

Over the Top!

During the Middle Ages, fashionable women in Japan were known to . . .

a. wear hats that were five feet tall.
b. blacken their teeth.
c. wear live cicadas in their hair.
d. have their feet bound to make them smaller.

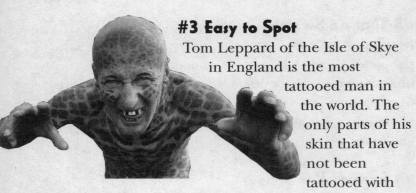

#3 Easy to Spot

Tom Leppard of the Isle of Skye in England is the most tattooed man in the world. The only parts of his skin that have not been tattooed with leopard spots are the insides of his ears and the skin between his toes.

#2 Piercing Habit

Elaine Davidson of Edinburgh, Scotland, holds the world record for the most body piercings—as of November 2003, she had 1,903 piercings. (*See color insert.*)

#1 Lizardman

Eric Sprague's love of reptiles prompted him to do his best to look like one. He had himself tattooed with scales from head to toe. These, along with his surgically split tongue and the bony ridge set into his forehead, have allowed him to achieve his goal.

Robert Ripley traveled the world seeking out unusual people. Here are our choices for the Top 10 Ripley Classics!

#10 Rubber Face

J. T. Saylors of Villa Rica, Georgia, was able to "swallow his nose." This unique skill is called girning—twisting one's features into an ugly face only a mother could love.

#9 Whoo, Whooo!

Martin Joe Laurello, also known as "The Human Owl," drew large crowds at Ripley's Odditoriums during the 1930s. His ability to swivel his head 180 degrees never failed to amaze.

Over the Top!

Every male in the Colombière family was born with . . .

a. six toes on each foot.
b. three ears.
c. four eyebrows.
d. two left hands.

#8 Bright Idea

The enterprising "Lighthouse Man" of Chunking, China, drilled a hole in his head and plugged it with a candle to light the way for visitors through the dark streets of his city.

#7 Small Wonder

Though he weighed a whopping nine pounds two ounces at birth in 1838, Charles Stratton never grew beyond three feet four inches tall. Discovered by P. T. Barnum and renamed "General Tom Thumb," Stratton became one of the biggest celebrities of his time, touring the United States and Europe.

#6 Head Case

In the 1930s, Lorraine Chevalier of Philadelphia, Pennsylvania, could sit on her own head. The famous Chevalier family of acrobats claimed that only one person is born into their family every 200 years who is capable of attaining this position.

#5 Fuzzy Was He

"Jo Jo the Dog-Faced Boy" suffered from a rare condition called hypertrichosis—also known as "werewolf syndrome"—which caused excess hair to grow all over his body. He toured in sideshows and carnivals and was a popular circus performer in the 1880s.

#4 The Human Unicorn

A Chinese farmer, known only as Weng, had a 13-inch horn growing out of the back of his head. Weng disappeared from view shortly after his photo was taken in Manchuria, China. Robert Ripley offered a reward to anyone who could find him again, but no one ever claimed the reward.

#3 Above It All

Robert Wadlow was an average-sized infant when he was born in 1918. However, by the time he reached age 22, he'd become the tallest person in recorded history, standing eight feet eleven inches tall.

#2 Triple Threat

In the 1930s, Francesco Lentini of Sicily, Italy, was a master musician. He was also a renowned soccer player. Perhaps having three legs contributed to his success on the field.

#1 Double Vision

Liu Ch'ung, governor of Shansi, China, was born in C.E. 955 with two pupils in each eye. Ch'ung was one of Ripley's all-time favorite "human oddities" and is one of the most popular wax figures in several Odditoriums.

Some people dare to be different in ways most of us would never even dream of. Get ready to meet our Top 10 Totally Flaky choices!

#10 Half-Baked

In the 1940s, John Pecinovsky of Iowa liked to do things by halves. He wore clothes of different colors on each side of his body—and a different haircut and shave on each side of his head.

Over the Top!

In the 18th century, Matthew Robinson of England regularly spent his entire day, including mealtimes, . . .

a. submerged up to his neck in the ocean.
b. smeared from head to toe with whale grease.
c. wearing only his underwear.
d. submerged in a vat of honey.

#9 R-eel-y Sad

Lucius Crassus (140–91 B.C.E.), a Roman law authority, was so fond of his trained lamprey eel that he gave it earrings and a pearl necklace. When the fish died, Crassus dressed in mourning clothes for an entire year!

13

#8 Jiminy Cricket!

A new game called "cricket spitting" was added to the 2003 annual Bug Bowl held at Rutgers University in New Brunswick, New Jersey. Contestants spit brown house crickets, roughly the size of watermelon seeds, as far as they could. First prize went to Chris O'Donovan, who spit his cricket 28 feet 5.75 inches.

#7 Shelled Out

Camillo Russo (left), of Melbourne, Australia, loved seashells so much that he used them to decorate his clothing and his home, which was covered with more than a million seashells.

#6 Suit Sower

Not one to let the grass grow under his feet, performance artist Gene Pool started a grass clothing line. He can grow an entire three-piece suit out of grass in just two weeks. Grass-covered cars are another of his specialties.

#5 King of the Road

After dressing up as Elvis one Halloween, cabdriver Dave Groh of Seattle, Washington, decided to wear his Elvis clothes every day. His tips improved, but he had to pay a 60-dollar fine for driving out of uniform!

Over the Top!

In his old age, celebrated French poet and priest Gaspard Abeille (1648–1718) had such amazing control of his facial wrinkles that he could use them to . . .

a. blindfold himself.
b. form the letters of the alphabet.
c. scare away dogs.
d. play a tune.

#4 Frog Feat

In the 1970s, Bill Steed, a professor of frog psychology at his own Croaker College, used hypnosis to train frogs to perform amazing feats, such as lifting barbells. (*See color insert.*)

#3 Beastly Welcome

Writer and naturalist Charles Waterton (1782–1864) sometimes slept outside in a tree with a sloth. He was also known to act like a dog, greeting his guests with a growl and scratching his head with his big toe.

#2 Junk Food

Michel Lotito, long considered a medical mystery, found that his unusual ability to chew and swallow indigestible household objects, such as razor blades, nuts, bolts, china, glasses, and cutlery, could be parlayed into a career. So far, he has ingested a grocery cart, a bicycle, a coffin, and a Cessna airplane.

#1 Cowboy Underpants

When Robert John Burck, who calls himself "The Naked Cowboy," takes to the streets of New York City, people stop and stare. That's because this street performer does his act wearing nothing but a cowboy hat, a pair of cowboy boots— and white underpants.

Ripley's Believe It or Not! Brain Buster

In a world full of oddities, fact often seems stranger than fiction. See if you can tell the difference between these freaky fibs and far-out facts.

Robert Ripley dedicated his life to seeking out the bizarre and unusual. But every unbelievable thing he recorded was proven to be true. In the Brain Buster at the end of every chapter, you'll play Ripley's role—trying to verify the fantastic facts presented. Each Ripley's Brain Buster contains a group of four shocking statements. But of these so-called "facts," **one** is **fiction.** Will you **Believe It!** or **Not!**?

Wait—there's more! Following the Brain Busters are special bonus questions where you can earn extra points! Keep score by flipping to the end of the book for the answer key and a scorecard.

Some people will do anything to get attention. Can you tell which show-offs are for real and which one is not?

a. In the 19th century, Jonathan James Toogood from Overblow, England, regularly jumped his horse over hedges while riding backward.

Believe It!   **Not!**

b. In 1942, Lena Deeter of Conway, Arkansas, amazed audiences by showing them how she could write with both hands in different directions—at the same time.

Believe It!   **Not!**

c. In 1956, 17-year-old Janetta Herman of Tuscaloosa, Alabama, was five feet ten inches tall but could squeeze her body into an urn 26 inches high and 18 inches wide.

Believe It!   **Not!**

d. In the 1920s, Joseph Darby of Dudley, England, could jump on an open basket of eggs and then leap off again with such lightning speed that he would not crack a single shell.

Believe It!   **Not!**

• •

BONUS QUESTION

Nothing can be stranger than the things that can go wrong with the human body. In 1978, 13-year-old Doug Pritchard of Lenoir, North Carolina, went to his doctor because . . .

a. a carrot was growing out of his ear.

b. he'd started growing an extra finger on each hand.

c. two extra pupils appeared in each eye.

d. a tooth was growing out of the bottom of his foot.

2 Critters

If you think of critters as "dumb animals," you're sure to change your mind when you read about our Top 10 Smart and Talented Animals!

#10 Purr-fect Eti-cat

When Faye Murrell's cat, Tessa, eats, she sits at the table. Most days, Tessa uses a fork or a spoon to eat her meals, but when noodles are served, she chows down with chopsticks.

Over the Top!

Porkchop is a pig who brings home the bacon when he performs tricks like . . .

a. jumping rope.
b. riding a skateboard.
c. juggling balls.
d. standing on his head.

#9 Trees to Skis

Twiggy the squirrel jets across the pool on skis while her owner uses a remote control to operate the miniature boat that pulls her.

#8 Paper Trail

In 1910, the Paris art critics gave high praise to Boronali's *Sunset on the Adriatic Sea*. Only later did they learn that Boronali was a donkey who painted with a brush tied to his tail.

#7 Jumping for Joy

Brutus is a dog with no fear of heights. In fact, he's never happier than when his owner, Ron Sirull, tucks him into a pouch on his chest and takes him skydiving.

#6 Trunk Show

To raise money for the Thai Elephant Conservation Center in Lampang, Thailand, conductors Richard Lair and Dave Soldier taught 12 elephants to play in an orchestra!

#5 Pig-casso

In 1998, Smithfield, a Vietnamese potbellied pig, began producing paintings that fetched hundreds of dollars each on eBay. Since then, he's earned 20,000 dollars through the sale of his art, all of which has been donated to charities.

#4 Crow's Feat

British researchers were surprised to find out that crows not only know how to use tools but also how to make them! They put a clear plastic tube containing corn kernels in with a caged crow and provided her with straight and curved wires. The crow chose the curved wire and retrieved her reward. When the crow was given a straight wire only, she used her beak to bend the wire so that the tool would work!

Over the Top!

Gary Wimer's dog, Isaac, knows how to . . .

a. predict the future.
b. paint beautiful pictures.
c. play ping pong.
d. multiply, divide, and do square roots.

#3 Math-panzee

One day, Dr. Sally Boysen, a scientist at Ohio State University, dropped three peaches in one box and three in another. She took out number cards and asked Sheba, a chimpanzee, how many peaches were in the boxes. Sheba pointed to six. Boysen was amazed. Sheba could recognize numbers, but had never been taught to count or add!

#2 Top Billing

Alex the parrot, trained by Professor Irene Pepperberg at Ohio State University, has a 100-word vocabulary. He can also identify 50 different objects and sort them by color, shape, and texture—proving that he is not merely "parroting" what he hears but processing information.

#1 Fetch!

Rico, a border collie in Germany, knows the names of 200 toys and will retrieve whichever one is asked for. During a test in which an unfamiliar object was mixed in with known objects, Rico associated the new word with the unfamiliar object. Four months later, with no further exposure to it, Rico recalled and singled out the new object from the others.

Animals can be pretty amazing—whether they're trained or acting on their own. Meet our picks for the Top 10 Awesome Animals!

#10 Techno Rat

When the cramped space above the ceiling made it impossible for Dr. Judy Reevis to wire a classroom to the Internet, she turned to a rat. After training, Rattie could pull 250 feet of cable through the crawl space, while Reevis tapped on the ceiling to keep him moving in the right direction.

Over the Top!

Arthur, an English setter belonging to Brian Revheim, has been trained to alert his family when . . .

a. Revheim is about to have an epileptic seizure.
b. someone trespasses on their property.
c. their toddler opens the garden gate.
d. deer invade the garden.

#9 No Horsing Around

Cuddles, a miniature horse just two feet tall, was the first

guide horse for the blind in the United States. Cuddles's training was put to the test when she and her owner, Dan Shaw, passed through New York City. Clad in tiny sneakers to prevent her from slipping, Cuddles took the busy streets and noisy subways right in stride.

#8 Scent-sational

Dog trainer Duane Pickel has trained a schnauzer named George to sniff out cancer before it can become a threat. After 8,000 hours of training, this talented canine correctly detected melanoma, the most dangerous form of skin cancer, 400 times out of 401 attempts!

#7 Splashing Around

In 1996, when a shark attacked Martin Richardson in the Red Sea, a few dolphins slapped the water with their fins and tails to keep the shark away until Richardson could be rescued.

#6 Winging It

A woman in Hermitage, Tennessee, who fell and cut her head, was rescued after her pet canary, Bibs, flew down the road to alert her niece. The bird kept tapping on the niece's window until she followed it to the accident scene.

Over the Top!

In February 2001, Flossie, a Labrador retriever–chow mix, awakened her famous owner just in time for her to escape a fire raging through the house. Who did Flossie save?

a. Britney Spears
b. Drew Barrymore
c. Julia Roberts
d. Gwyneth Paltrow

#5 He-roo

A baby kangaroo rescued by Nigel Etherington of Perth, Australia, later saved Etherington from a fire by banging its tail on his door until he awoke and escaped.

#4 Canine Lifeline

On December 10, 1919, the S.S. *Ethie*, a 414-ton steamship, ran aground off Newfoundland, Canada, during a violent storm. With the ship breaking up in the heavy seas, the captain couldn't launch the lifeboats— but all was not lost. A Newfoundland dog gripped a lifeline in his teeth and swam to the beach, where a bystander secured the line, and all 92 passengers and crew were pulled to safety.

#3 One Great Ape

A silverback gorilla named Jambo came to the rescue when five-year-old Levan Merritt fell into the gorilla compound at England's Jersey Zoo, keeping the other gorillas away while comforting the boy until help arrived.

#2 Saved by a Bullet

In 2000, the Sica family paid 5,000 dollars on surgery to

save the life of Bullet, their 13-year-old golden retriever. Two years later, Bullet repaid the favor by alerting the Sicas when their three-week-old son began to choke. Had the paramedics arrived just ten seconds later, the baby would have died.

#1 What a Pig!

When Jo Altsman of Beaver Falls, Pennsylvania, had a heart attack, her pet potbellied pig, Lulu, squeezed through a doggy door and ran out into the street. Then she lay down and played dead to attract help—and ultimately saved her owner's life.

Are you ready for some strange animal stories? You'll find them in our choices for the Top 10 Offbeat Animals.

#10 Getting Rat-tled

Rat breeder Steffany Heller of Harrisburg, Pennsylvania, usually has at least 75 rats in her home. In 1999, even her seven-month-old daughter was partial to Socrates, a dumbo rat, whose large, low-set ears give the species its name.

#9 Slime Time

Carl Bramham not only keeps snails as pets but also trains them to compete in races. In July 1995, Archie, his most-prized racer, won the annual World Snail Racing Championship held in Congham, England. Archie, beating out 150 other snails, set a world record of two minutes and 20 seconds to go the distance—of 13 inches!

Over the Top!

Hunter York is the proud owner of Mary-Kate and Ashley, his . . .

a. twin alpacas.
b. two capuchin monkeys.
c. pair of scarlet macaws.
d. two-headed king snake.

#8 Leapin' Lizards

Henry Lizardlover has parlayed his hobby of keeping iguanas into a thriving business, featuring a line of cards that picture his 30 iguanas in humanlike poses. Here, Prince Charming gives his pal Tallulah a ride on his bike.

#7 Lionhearted

Lions love a type of antelope called an oryx—at mealtime, that is. That's why scientists are puzzled by the behavior of a lioness named Kamuniak on the Samburu National Reserve in Kenya. Since January 1992, Kamuniac has been scaring off mother oryx and adopting their babies, catching food for them and protecting them from other big cats.

#6 Puppy Love

When Kia, an endangered subspecies of chimpanzee known as a bonobo, was born in 2002 at the Twycross Zoo near Birmingham, England, she was rejected by the other bonobos. So the zoo's director took her home, where her bulldog, Bugsy, showered her new roommate with sloppy kisses!

#5 Watertight

In 1998, Dan Heath of Medford, Oregon, spotted his dog, Chino, standing over a fishpond nose-to-nose with Falstaff, a carp. Heath doesn't know how the two became friends, but every day, Chino sprints out to the backyard and peers into the water. Soon Falstaff pops up, and the two gently touch noses!

#4 Got a Spare?

Farmer Rob Adriaans from Nuenen, Holland, was sure the ewe (female sheep) he was assisting in childbirth was about to have twins. Imagine his surprise when there was only one healthy baby lamb—one baby lamb with six legs, that is!

Over the Top!

A mixed-up male swan that lives in a pond in Hamburg, Germany, has fallen head over tail feathers for a . . .

a. statue of a swan.
b. goose.
c. swan-shaped boat.
d. great egret.

#3 Roach Catchers

In Australia, some people keep cockroaches as pets. However, these are not just ordinary cockroaches but wingless Australian burrowing cockroaches—and they're as big as the palm of a hand!

#2 Glow Figure

Get ready to meet the first designer pets from Yorktown Technologies in Texas. Called GloFish, these flashy zebrafish have been genetically engineered by Zhiyuan Gong to be the same fluorescent red color as a sea coral.

#1 Two-faced

No, you're not seeing double. Image the kitten was born in June 2000 in Bensalem, Pennsylvania, with one head but two faces! Since Image has just one brain, both faces blink, yawn, and sneeze at the same time.

The courage of animals in the face of danger should never be underestimated. Can you spot the beastly impostor among the three furry heroes?

a. Joleen Walderbach's German shepherd, Shelby, was named Skippy Dog Hero of the Year after he saved Walderbach's parents and two neighbor children from carbon monoxide poisoning by nudging and barking at them until they left the house.

Believe It! **Not!**

b. When the home of the Billings family of Briarcliff, New Jersey, was about to be robbed, their two pet squirrels jumped from a tree onto the thief's head, biting and scratching him until the police arrived.

Believe It! **Not!**

c. In 1961, a pod of dolphins protected a group of shipwrecked sailors from circling sharks off the coast of Florida.

Believe It! **Not!**

d. In 1995, Priscilla the pig became the first animal to be inducted into the Texas Veterinary Medical Association's Hall of Fame after she saved 11-year-old Anthony Melton from drowning in a lake near Houston.

Believe It! **Not!**

BONUS QUESTION

Animals are often capable of excelling in ways that scientists once thought were exclusively human. Test your critter smarts by identifying the statement that is not true.

a. An octopus at Ripley's Aquarium in South Carolina figured out how to open its tank, crawl out, and eat the fish in the next tank, then return to its own tank and close it, fooling everyone until it was finally caught in the act.

b. While working in his lab at Bowling Green State University, Professor Jaak Panksepp made an unusual discovery: Rats laugh when they're tickled.

c. Stanley Curtis at Pennsylvania State University has taught pigs to play video games.

d. Justine Geste, a marine biologist at Florida State University, has taught a mako shark to sing.

There are people who will try anything—and here to prove it are our Top 10 choices in the What a Stunt! category.

Over the Top!

Birdie Tilman crossed a tightrope above Times Square in New York City while . . .

a. riding a unicycle.
b. balancing a basketful of eggs on her head.
c. playing an accordion.
d. hanging by her mouth from a bar attached to the rope.

#10 One Cool Dude

In November 2000, street magician David Blaine spent just under 62 hours inside a six-ton block of ice on the corner of 44th Street and Broadway in New York City.

#9 Up on the Housetops

In free running, an extreme sport invented by Sebastien Foucan, participants scale buildings, run along narrow ledges, and jump from rooftop to rooftop. Foucan even used a battleship in London, England, as a springboard for his leaps.

#8 You Go, Girl!

Shannon Pole Summer was only 14 years old when she pulled a truck packed with members of a high school football team—a combined weight of 12,720 pounds—for 100 feet!

#7 Skywalker

On November 11, 1998, Jay Cochrane crossed a tightrope 30 stories above the ground that was stretched 600 feet between the two towers of the Flamingo Hilton hotel in Las Vegas—while blindfolded!

#6 Chairman of the Board

Tony Hawk can do a spine-tingling 900-degree trick in which he spins two and half times in the air while holding on to his skateboard. He is also master of the 720-degree trick in which

he and his board spin completely around twice and land backward. So far, no one else has been able to duplicate either of these moves.

#5 Head Trip

Gao Fu Zhoa helped usher in the Year of the Snake in a most unusual way. On January 9, 2001, the 50-year-old performer from China fed a 25-inch-long snake through his own nostril, down his throat, and out of his mouth.

Over the Top!

Iron Man Sultan Beybars of Egypt (1223–1277) swam across the Nile River and back every day for 17 years while . . .

a. wearing a suit of armor and dragging a 38-pound weight.

b. pulling a camel on a raft.

c. carrying a tame 200-pound alligator on his back.

d. pulling a boat full of children by a rope grasped in his teeth.

#4 Hooked on Danger

Criss Angel, a magician, once spent six hours dangling from a ceiling by fishhooks pushed through the skin of his back and legs.

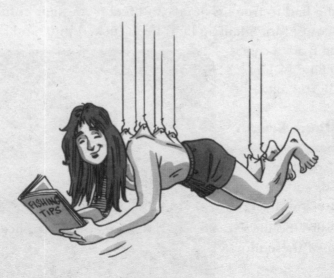

#3 A Flying Leap

BASE jumpers leap off fixed structures such as buildings, which are usually less than 1,000 feet tall. Once airborne, the jumpers free-fall, often deploying their parachutes only 10 to 15 seconds from the ground. In January 2004, 53 BASE jumpers leaped from the top of the Petronas Towers in Kuala Lumpur, Malaysia, the second tallest building in the world.

#2 Death Dive

After he was dropped from a plane, escape artist Robert Gallup had 60 seconds to deploy his parachute—but first, he had to free his hands and feet from their cuffs, break out of the mailbag he'd been tucked into, and escape from a cage by picking its lock! Luckily, he made it.

#1 Mouse Breath

Dagmarr Rothman could swallow a live mouse, wait for a minute, and bring it up unharmed from his stomach!

No doubt you've seen or heard about things that are truly yucky—but wait till you read about our Top 10 Totally Gross picks!

#10 Petrified Puke

One day, 160 million years ago, an ichthyosaur threw up. How do we know? In 2002, paleontologists found 160-million-year-old fossilized vomit in an English quarry.

Over the Top!

Durian is a popular fruit grown in Southeast Asia that smells so foul . . .

a. restaurants serve it in specially ventilated rooms.
b. it is banned from many hotels and buses.
c. in some countries, it's used to quell riots.
d. it was once used by police to extract confessions from criminals who couldn't stand being exposed to it.

#9 Good Grub

In Washington, D.C., during the early 1990s, The Insect Club was a popular restaurant. A typical meal consisted of fried mealworms for an appetizer, roasted Australian grubs and worm balls in spicy tomato sauce as the entrée, and cricket brittle for dessert.

#8 Sluggish Market
One of the biggest sellers at Fugetsudo, a popular sweet shop in Japan, is sea-slug ice cream.

#7 Pop Go the Crickets
In June 2003, an invasion of Mormon crickets appeared and covered almost every square inch of Elko, Nevada.

After thousands of the 2.5-inch-long insects were squashed by cars, the highways got so slippery that electronic overhead signs were programmed to alert motorists to slow down.

#6 Surprise!
When a chunk of ice crashed through the skylight of Ray Erickson's boat, he couldn't figure out where it came from. When the ice thawed, however, there was no mistaking what it was— toilet waste that had been released by an airplane!

#5 Strong Coffee
Some consider luak coffee from Indonesia the best. How does it get that way? When the luak, a relative of the bobcat, eats the fruit of the best coffee plants, it digests the husks but not the beans. People gather up piles of luak manure to harvest the beans—which are improved by their trip through the animal's digestive system!

#4 Living Jewels

In the Yucatán peninsula of Mexico, people use ma'kech beetles for jewelry. They apply nontoxic glue to the beetles' tough outer wings and affix decorative stones. Then they add a little gold ring and attach a chain leading to a brooch so the critter can crawl around but not escape.

Over the Top!

In 1995, a train on the Casablanca–Fez railroad line in Morocco slipped off the rails after . . .

a. a horde of snails slimed the tracks.
b. thousands of crushed locusts slimed the train's wheels.
c. an overturned truck spilled raw, slimy sewage on the tracks.
d. an oil spill slimed the tracks.

#3 Pooper-scoopers

Dung beetles scout out fresh mammal droppings and roll the dung into a ball. Then they poke a hole in it and lay their eggs inside. When the eggs hatch, the larvae have to eat through the dung to get out.

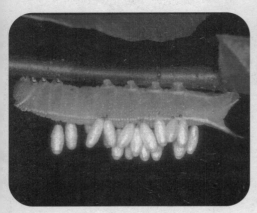

#2 Dining In

A parasitic wasp injects its eggs into a living caterpillar. After hatching, the wasp larvae eat their host alive, then burst through its skin, leaving nothing but cocoons behind.

#1 On the Fly

A special kind of cheese called *casu marzu* is made in Sardinia, Italy, by covering a lump of pecorino cheese with cheesecloth and leaving it outside. It attracts barn flies, which lay their eggs in the cheese. Before long, it's swarming with maggots, which produce enzymes that help break down the fats. Sardinians eat it, maggots and all, and consider it delicious. Most everyone else considers it *casu marzu*—rotten cheese!

If you haven't already been grossed out, read all about our choices for Top 10 Body Bits!

#10 Achoo!

Run for cover! Here's an amazingly gross though little-known fact: The drops of moisture in a sneeze can travel up to 150 feet per second. That's 102 miles per hour!

#9 Crazy Cures

If you happened to become ill in Louisiana during the 1800s, several popular "cures" just might have made you sicker. A tea made of cockroaches was a remedy for tetanus, and cockroaches fried in oil and garlic were used to cure indigestion. *Burp!*

Over the Top!

An early remedy for whooping cough was to have a patient . . .

a. roll in cow dung.
b. eat boiled mouse brains.
c. put a live frog in his or her mouth.
d. eat maggot cheese.

#8 Hard to Stomach

In 1822, a Canadian named Alexis St. Martin was accidentally shot in the stomach. When his stomach healed, he still had a gaping six-inch hole in his side, but his doctor, William Beaumont, made the best of it. He tied bits of food onto strings, put them through the hole, and periodically pulled the food out to examine it—thereby discovering the secrets of digestion!

#7 Maggot Medicine

Maggots, nature's tiniest microsurgeons, are used as a last resort when conventional medical treatments have failed and amputation is the only option. Bred in a special lab, the maggots clean wounds by eating dead tissue and harmful bacteria. There's only one catch—they have to be removed within 72 hours or they'll turn into flies.

#6 Don't Forget to Floss!

Too small to see without a microscope but not too small to smell, bacteria are a major source of bad breath—and you have about a hundred million of them in your mouth! Even after brushing, each tooth is still host to about 100,000 of these tiny creatures!

#5 Room Spray

With each flush of the toilet, hundreds of thousands of microscopic water droplets hit the air—and each and every one of them is filled with intestinal bacteria. Better keep that toothbrush tucked safely in a drawer!

#4 Five Dead Mice

Some people in China drink an elixir called Mice Saki to cure colds and a variety of aches and pains. The manufacturer guarantees a full refund if five individual mice are not visible floating around inside the bottle.

Over the Top!

In 12th-century Europe, a medicine was made from . . .

a. sheep's urine.
b. pureed garden slugs.
c. tea made from crushed cockroaches.
d. boiled Egyptian mummy skin and wrappings.

#3 Eye Strain

Having trouble keeping your eyes open? Maybe it's because hundreds of microscopic creatures, called follicle mites, are tucked into the roots of your eyelashes!

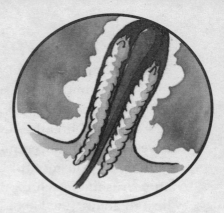

#2 Mite-y Dedication

Veterinarian Robert A. Lopez of Westport, New York, transplanted ear mites from cats' ears to his own! What did he find out? The host can feel and hear the mites as they scurry around the ear canal.

#1 Cut It Out!

An Israeli woman was cleaning house when a cockroach flew into her mouth. When she tried to pry it out of her throat with a fork, she swallowed both the roach and the fork. An X-ray showed that the fork was wedged sideways

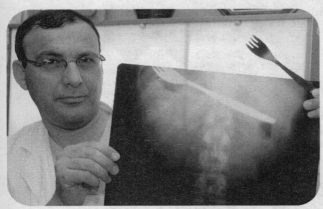

in her stomach. She had surgery to remove the fork—but the roach had already been digested.

Brain Buster

Extreme stunts require intensive training and lots of backup—and, oh yes, a daredevil with personality. Only three of the stunts listed below have been performed. Can you spot the one that has yet to be attempted?

a. On January 22, 2003, Ruth Rheinardsen of Milwaukee, Wisconsin, dove through a hole in the ice of Lake Michigan and swam 165 feet before coming back out.
Believe It!   **Not!**

b. On May 4, 1998, Mike Howard walked across an aluminum bar stretched between two hot-air balloons floating more than three miles above the town of Marshall, Michigan.
Believe It!   **Not!**

c. Tim Cridland used pain-deadening meditation before lying down on a bed of nails and allowing a 3,000-pound vehicle to drive over him.
Believe It!   **Not!**

d. Canadian unicyclist Kris Holm rode within four inches of a 2,000-foot-high cliff and leaped six feet across a crevasse thousands of feet deep.
Believe It!   **Not!**

BONUS QUESTION

Throughout history, ailing people have been willing to do some pretty disgusting things to make themselves feel better. In England during the 1850s, . . .

a. cockroaches fried in oil with garlic were used to cure cases of indigestion.

b. people believed that kissing a mouse was a surefire way to get rid of a cough.

c. a treatment for deafness was to pour the blood of a mole into the patient's ear.

d. a remedy for chicken pox was to eat three tablespoons of mashed rooster brains.

CHAPTER 4 Creepy!

When a person dies, something has to be done with the corpse.
Here are our nominations for the Top 10 Good-byes!

#10 Quicky Farewell

Between nine o'clock and midnight, mourners in a hurry can use the drive-in lane of the G. W. Thompson Chapel of Remembrance in Spartanburg, South Carolina, to stop for a moment by the casket in the picture window and pay their respects!

Over the Top!

A large statue tops the grave of Manfred Asho, a wealthy native of Cameroon who died in 1933. Next to it . . .

a. is a table on which a daily meal is served for his soul.
b. are statues of his wife and six children.
c. is his favorite fishing boat.
d. is a life-sized marble statue of his favorite horse.

#9 All Bottled Up

When a person died in 19th-century Borneo, the body was squeezed into a jar and kept in the house of a relative for a year.

#8 Going Out with a Bang

Celebrate Life, a company located in California, will scatter a deceased person's ashes in a spectacular fireworks display launched from a barge called *Heaven Sent*. Some of the themes you can choose from are "Knocking on Heaven's Door," "Stairway to Heaven," and "When Irish Eyes Are Smiling."

#7 For Environmentalists Only

Eternal Reefs, Inc., of Atlanta, Georgia, will mix a deceased person's ashes with concrete to form a "reef ball," which will then be submerged in the ocean to become an artificial reef for undersea life.

#6 Space Cadets

In 1997, the ashes of *Star Trek* creator Gene Roddenberry and 23 other people were blasted into space on board a Pegasus rocket that will circle Earth for years.

#5 Sparkling Tribute

When 80-year-old Edna MacArthur of Alberta, Canada, died in 2002, her family had her turned into a diamond and set in a gold ring! The transformation involves cremating the body and compressing the ashes into a small cube. The cube is subjected to intense heat to convert it into carbon, then crafted into a synthetic diamond.

#4 Eternal Vigilance

War Eagle, chief of the Yankton Sioux Indians, was

buried in Sioux City, Iowa, sitting on his horse. With his eyes just above the surface of the ground, he could continue to overlook his old hunting grounds.

#3 Good Spirits
In Brazil, the Uape people of the upper Amazon drank the ashes of their cremated dead mixed with *casiri,* a local alcoholic beverage, in the belief they would absorb all the good qualities of the deceased.

#2 Car-cass
In 1998, at the age of 84, Rose Martin of Tiverton, Massachusetts, died and was buried in her 1962 Corvair. She'd bought it new for 2,500 dollars and had decided she wanted to be with it always.

#1 On the Fly
In 2002, "Steady" Ed Headrick, the inventor who helped perfect the Frisbee and invented disc golf, died at age 78 in California. True to his wishes, his family had his ashes incorporated into special memorial discs. Limited edition sets from the Disc Golf Association come with two disks—one to play with and one to keep—for 210 dollars. Proceeds go into a nonprofit memorial fund.

If you thought some of the Good-bye stories were weird, wait till you have a look at our Top 10 Really Freaky choices!

#10 Flower Power

'Abbad al-Mu'tadid, who ruled Seville, Spain, from 1042 to 1069, used the skulls of his enemies as planters for flowers.

#9 Skullduggery

Among Robert Ripley's souvenirs are skulls from New Guinea, long ago taken by warriors as trophies. The skulls of honored relatives were also kept, covered with clay, and decorated.

Over the Top!

On November 16, 1667, Dorothy Ford was married to William Streat of South Pool, England. What was unusual about their wedding?

a. The groom was a corpse.
b. The bride dressed in black.
c. The bride and groom were English cocker spaniels.
d. The couple took their vows in the tomb of the bride's dead parents.

Trophy skull

Ancestor skull

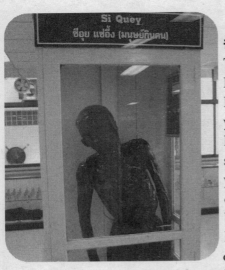

#8 Freaky Forensics

The founder of the Forensic Museum in Bangkok, Thailand, greets you at the door. Well, not him exactly—just his skeleton. Continue on and you will see an assortment of body parts, bleeding brains, skulls with bullet holes, severed arms, a set of lungs with stab wounds, and even the mummy of a serial killer!

#7 Body Art

German professor Gunther von Hagens has created an elaborate public anatomy lesson with his traveling exhibit of donated human corpses in active poses, such as running and playing games. The bodies, minus their skin, are preserved by *plastination,* a process that involves replacing bodily fluids with plastics. (*See color insert.*)

#6 Show-and-Tell

In 1997, pathologist Dr. Thomas Harvey placed the brain of Albert Einstein in a plastic container and drove it from Florida to California to show it to the dead scientist's granddaughter.

#5 Handy Tool

In medieval England, a mummified hand, cut from the body of a hanged man, was carried by burglars, who believed that it could open locked doors.

Over the Top!

After England's Sir Walter Raleigh was beheaded in 1618, his wife, Elizabeth, buried his body but . . .

a. used his skull as a doorstop.
b. kept his embalmed head in a bag for the last 29 years of her life.
c. donated his mummified head to the British Museum.
d. kept his skull on the mantle of the fireplace in her bedroom.

#4 Finger Bowl

The middle finger from the right hand of Galileo (1546–1642), astronomer and inventor of the telescope, is on display in a bowl at the Museum of the History of Science in Florence, Italy.

#3 Queen of Hearts

Queen Marguerite de Valois (1552–1615) of Navarre, Spain, had pockets sewn into the lining of her voluminous hoopskirt to hold the hearts of her 34 successive sweethearts, each embalmed and sealed in a separate box!

#2 Keeping Their Heads

The Jivaro, a warlike people of South America, believed that to decapitate an enemy and possess his head was to keep for one's self all the powers of its original owner. Not only did warriors keep an enemy's head, they also shrank it to about the size of a baseball.

#1 Graveyard Bash

Every five years, people who live in Madagascar observe a sacred ritual called Famadihana. Families remove their dead relatives from their tombs, catch them up on family news, and even dance with the dead bodies before sitting down to a lavish banquet. Afterward, the corpses are given new shrouds and returned to their tombs.

Do you believe in the supernatural? See if you feel the same way after reading about our picks for the Top 10 Seriously Spooky category!

#10 Stiff Competition

Spirits live in Cassadaga, a tiny Florida town of about 100 people founded by George Colby in 1898 as a refuge for mediums, astrologers, and other spiritual counselors. Today all the (living) residents are psychics, many of whom are certified mediums, whose main business is communicating with the dead.

Over the Top!

In 1683, religious leader Roger Williams was buried next to an apple tree in Providence, Rhode Island. Over time, the . . .

a. roots of the tree slowly absorbed his body and assumed a human shape.
b. tree stopped producing fruit.
c. tree toppled over onto his grave.
d. apple blossoms appeared even though it was midwinter.

#9 Haunted Highway

From 1984 to 1990, there were 519 car accidents along a 40-mile stretch of Alabama highway. Locals believe that the road is haunted by the ghosts of the Native Americans who are buried there.

#8 Ghostly Image

Of course there's no such thing as a ghost . . . but then who is that standing behind Mary Todd Lincoln in this photo taken many years after Abraham Lincoln's death? Is it Lincoln's ghost? An optical illusion? A fake?

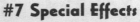

#7 Special Effects

Even though no one is there, family members often hear children running and laughing on the third floor of the Arlington House in Virginia, which was once lived in by Robert E. Lee.

#6 Spirited Uproars

Catherine Howard was beheaded by her husband, King Henry VIII, in 1542, so why do the servants at Hampton Court in England swear that she still roams the castle? It must be the bloodcurdling screams that come from her old rooms.

Editor's Top 10 Pics

#10 Dead Man Playing

German professor Gunther von Hagens has created an elaborate public anatomy lesson with his traveling exhibit of donated human corpses in active poses. The bodies, minus their skin, are preserved by *plastination,* a process that involves replacing bodily fluids with plastics. Checkmate!

#9 Ribbet-ing Performance

In the 1970s, Bill Steed, a professor of frog psychology at his own Croaker College, used hypnosis to train frogs to perform amazing feats, such as weight-lifting.

#8 Hard Pressed

Invented in 1997 by Phil Shaw, extreme ironing takes ironing to new heights. Here, Mat "Starch" Scull gets in some practice before starting off on the 2004 Rowenta Extreme Ironing tour in the United States.

#7 Cheek-a-bob

At the annual Vegetarian Festival in Phuket, Thailand, participants skewer themselves instead of the food. They puncture their cheeks with knives, skewers, and other implements. Ouch!

Bonified Retreat

When a Czech cemetery filled up in 1511, monks dug up and stored the bones. In 1870, a woodcarver was hired to do something about them—and now the bones of 40,000 people bedeck the chapel from top to bottom

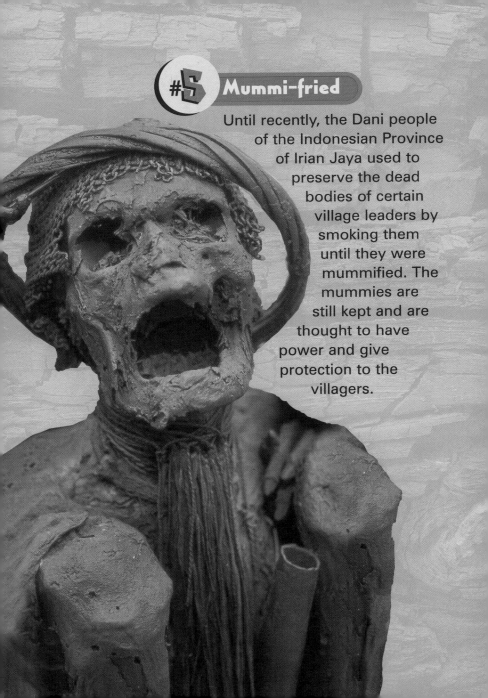

#5 Mummi-fried

Until recently, the Dani people of the Indonesian Province of Irian Jaya used to preserve the dead bodies of certain village leaders by smoking them until they were mummified. The mummies are still kept and are thought to have power and give protection to the villagers.

#4 **Milking It!**

Bowls of milk and food are scattered throughout the Karni Mata Temple in India for the rats that live there. Many people believe the rats carry the souls of storytellers and, when they die, will come back as people.

#3 Bee-Wear

Bee charmer Norman Gary attracted 60,000 bees to land on his body. What did he do next? He serenaded them with sweet music, of course!

#2 Sharper Image

As of November 2003, Elaine Davidson of Edinburgh, Scotland, had 1,903 piercings—a world record!

Lizard of Odds

Eric Sprague loves reptiles.
That's why he had himself
made over to look like
a lizard—complete with
head-to-toe-tattoos,
a forked tongue, and
a bony ridge implanted
in his forehead.

#5 Ship of Ghouls

From her maiden voyage in 1936, to her final one in the late 1950s, about 50 people perished aboard the *Queen Mary*. Today, the ship is a floating hotel in Long Beach, California, and guests staying there have reported seeing the ghosts of these casualties in such areas as the indoor first-class pool, the royal theater, and the boiler room, as well as on the decks. The hotel even offers a Ghost Encounters Tour of the ship!

Over the Top!

In the Gardens of Marius in Rome, Italy, a 120-foot-tall portrait of the Roman emperor Nero was struck and destroyed by lightning on the very day in 68 C.E. that . . .

a. Rome began to burn.
b. the Roman army invaded Greece.
c. Nero took his own life in a villa four miles away.
d. Nero had his own mother, Agrippina, murdered.

#4 Mourning Pigeon

Something strange marked the burial service for Captain Joseph Belain. As if in tribute to the man who had dedicated his life to saving the carrier pigeon from extinction, a carrier pigeon flew in, perched on the bier, and stayed until the service was over.

#3 Spirit of Revenge

Thirty years after having killed a man on the island of Malta, celebrated sculptor Melchiore Caffa (c. 1631–1667) created a statue of his victim to mark his grave. While Caffa was putting the final touches on the sculpture, it toppled over and crushed him to death.

#2 Trunk-ated Engagement

The schooner *Susan and Eliza* was wrecked in a storm off Cape Ann, Massachusetts. Aboard was the shipowner's daughter, Susan Hichborn, on her way to her wedding in Boston. All 33 passengers perished, and no trace of the ship was ever found, except for a trunk containing Hichborn's possessions and bearing her initials. The trunk washed ashore at the feet of her waiting fiancé.

#1 Going Nowhere

In her 160-room mansion in San Jose, California, Sarah Winchester had stairways built that run into the ceiling, and doors that open onto blank walls. Why? To soothe the spirits of people who were killed by rifles made by her late husband's family.

Ripley's Believe It or Not Brain Buster

It's time to test your knowledge of the eerily bizarre and the unbelievably creepy. Three of these Ripley's oddities are documented truth. Can you tell which one is fully fictitious?

a. In World War I, a British observation plane on the western front flew in wide circles for several hours and then landed without mishap—even though its pilot and observer were both dead.

Believe It!   **Not!**

b. As a joke, Edward Moore, an English dramatist, sent his own obituary to the newspapers on February 27, 1757, giving the next day as his date of death—and on February 28, he suddenly became ill and died.

Believe It!   **Not!**

c. Imelda Marcos threw a party in honor of her late husband's 73rd birthday. The former president of the Philippines attended but was not very good company, since he arrived frozen in his casket.

Believe It!   **Not!**

d. When a person of Transylvanian descent dies, his or her children inherit a sealed urn full of the blood of the loved one.

Believe It!   **Not!**

BONUS QUESTION

Everybody dies, but not every body is buried. When his grandfather died, Trygve Bauge, then of Nederland, Colorado, had the body . . .

a. cremated and the ashes scattered in a spectacular fireworks display.

b. mummified in the style of ancient Egypt and placed in a one-quarter scale replica of the Great Pyramid of Cheops.

c. cryogenically preserved in nitrogen and stored in a shed regularly stocked with dry ice to keep it cold until the day science comes up with a way to bring his grandpa back to life.

d. cremated and the ashes sent to the Moon on a Lunar Prospector spacecraft.

All around the globe, people practice different rituals and folkways. Here are our picks for the Top 10 Offbeat Customs!

#10 Earth Tones

In Caryville, Florida, there is an annual International Worm Fiddling contest in which contestants play music to draw earthworms out of the soil.

Over the Top!

In India during the spring festival of Holi, partygoers use tubes called *pichkaris* to. . .

a. spray colored water all over each other.
b. play sacred music.
c. scatter flowers in front of the temples.
d. paint sacred portraits.

#9 Balancing Act

Every year, women of the Balanta tribe, in Guinea-Bissau, Africa, perform a dance with huge baskets containing their husbands or sweethearts balanced on their heads!

#8 Food Fight

Every August in the town of Buñol, Spain, 20,000 people celebrate the annual harvest with a festival called La Tomatina—which ends in the world's biggest tomato fight! The streets become slippery with splattered tomatoes, and it isn't long before everyone looks like they've just taken a bath in marinara sauce.

#7 Daredevils

Since 1620, the town of Castrillo de Murcia in Spain has celebrated the holiday of Corpus Christi with a baby-jumping festival! During the festival, a man called "El Colacho" dresses up in a yellow-and-red costume and leaps over babies born in the previous year. Why? El Colacho represents the devil, and it's said that as he jumps, he takes evil with him, leaving the infants cleansed of original sin.

#6 Lousy Choice

In 19th-century Sweden, a new burgomaster was chosen by placing a louse in the center of a table. The man whose beard the insect jumped into held the office for the next year.

#5 Just Spit It Out

It's considered good manners in Kenya for Masai warriors to spit at each other when they meet.

#4 Fairest of All!

Each year, the Wodaabe people of West Africa hold beauty contests for men. Bedecked with special makeup, jewelry, charms, and elaborate costumes, the men dance for days to impress the judges, who are two or three beautiful women. Each judge chooses a winner. What does he get as a prize? The judge as his bride!

#3 Scent-sational

A tribal custom in New Guinea takes some of the stink out of saying good-bye. Close friends and relatives stick their fingers in each other's armpits and rub the scent on themselves so that they'll have a fragrant reminder of their loved ones after parting.

#2 Horsing around!

For centuries, a grueling cross-country race has been staged during the annual Naadam Festival in Mongolia to determine the country's fastest horses. Hundreds of horses compete in a mad dash over an 18-mile-long course—all of them ridden by children ages four to twelve!

#1 Leap of Faith

The Land Divers of Pentecost, an island in the South Pacific, jump headfirst from an 80-foot-tall tower with only vines attached to their ankles to keep them from smashing into the ground. Why do they do it? It's a coming-of-age ritual, with boys as young as eight years old making their first jump.

It's hard to say whether Mother Nature or humans come up with the most fantastic constructions. See if you agree with our picks for the Top 10 Most Peculiar Places!

#10 Cheers!

Marvelously wrought in stone by the lathe-work action of the wind, the 15-foot-high Goblet of Venus in San Juan County, Utah, stood on a base just ten inches wide—before it was destroyed by vandals in the 1940s, that is.

#9 Most Breakable

Tressa "Grandma" Prisbrey visited the dump every day from 1951 to 1981, picking up discarded bottles to build Bottle Village, a fantasy of shrines, wishing wells, child-sized buildings—and even a Leaning Tower of Bottle Village—all made of glass bottles.

Over the Top!

It took 40 years for Baldasare Forestiere to build his 90-room Fresno, California, home—a one-of-a-kind house built . . .

a. out of used tires.
b. entirely underground.
c. around a skating rink.
d. on stilts.

#8 Jet-sitters

Marcus Sitticus, the 17th-century prince-archbishop of Salzburg, Austria, had water jets installed on the stools around his palace courtyard in order to surprise his unsuspecting guests. Four hundred years later, the water jets still work!

#7 Rock Music

Covering 3.5 acres, the Great Stalacpipe Organ in the Luray Caverns of Virginia is the largest musical instrument in the world. Built in 1954, the organ uses natural stalactites instead of metal pipes to make music. Its creator, Leland Sprinkle, a mathematician and scientist, chose stalactites that would perfectly match the musical scale.

Over the Top!

The Koutoubia, an 800-year-old tower in Marrakesh, Morocco, was built with mortar mixed with . . .

a. crushed quartz crystals so that it would sparkle in the sun.
b. the crushed bones of the city's holy men after they died.
c. sand believed to have been tread upon by Mohammed.
d. 900 bags of musk so that it would always smell like perfume.

#6 Gift from the Sea

A small but beautiful chapel on the Isle of Guernsey in Great Britain is made entirely of seashells.

#5 Headquarters

The inside of the octagonal Armour-Stiner house in Irvington, New York, represents a human brain. Its rooms were laid out according to the principles of phrenology, the pseudoscience that maintains that bumps on the head have an effect on personality.

#4 Fish out of Water

Built in the shape of a fish, the National Fresh Water Fishing Hall of Fame & Museum in Hayward, Wisconsin, is half a city-block long and four-and-a-half stories tall.

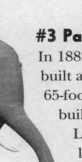

#3 Pachyderm Pavilion

In 1882, James T. Lafferty built a hotel shaped like a 65-foot-tall elephant. The building, nicknamed Lucy, is now a historic landmark in Margate, New Jersey.

#2 Rock Solid

While delivering mail in rural France in 1879, Ferdinand Cheval stumbled over a fancifully eroded stone. Inspired by its beauty, Cheval decided to construct a home from the same material. It took him 33 years to create Le Palais Idéal, a four-story, 86-foot-long castle covered with intricate carvings of animals, plants, and people.

#1 That's Odd!

Noted for their totally outrageous architecture, Ripley's Believe It or Not! Odditoriums can be found all across America and in many other countries as well. Each one features hundreds of unbelievable exhibits, incredible illusions, and

film clips of amazing stunts, such as Dagmarr Rothman swallowing a mouse and bringing it back up unharmed.

We all have the urge to create art—it just takes different, sometimes strange, forms. Open your mind and take a look at our choices for the Top 10 Crazy Creations!

#10 Scrap-o-saurus

Jim Garry of Farmingdale, New Jersey, creates detailed dinosaur skeletons out of old car parts.

Over the Top!

Artist Wu Luo Zhong creates beautiful sculptures out of . . .

a. peanut butter.
b. toilet paper.
c. wasps' nests.
d. chewing gum.

#9 Hair Piece

Artist Manuel Andrada of Ecuador painted a microscopic version of *The Last Supper* on a grain of rice using hairs from the back of his hand for paintbrushes.

#8 Burning Passion
Tadhiko Okawa recreated Da Vinci's *Mona Lisa* and other classic works of art from pieces of strategically burned toast.

#7 A Lot of Fluff
Slater Barron of Long Beach, California, creates life-size sculptures, murals, and portraits (left) out of laundry lint.

#6 Pedal Picker
In 1981, Ray Nelson of San Jose, California, built a fully functional motorcycle in the shape of an electric guitar, which he's ridden from California to New York City.

#5 Shooting the Works

In the 1930s, Ernie and Dot Lind were known for the bullet-hole art they created by shooting at canvases rather than painting them.

#4 Lid Flipper

Plumber Barney Smith has a private museum with more than 500 works of art created on discarded toilet seats. Just about anything can become material for his one-of-a-kind creations— eyeglasses, pill bottles, marbles, and even beehives.

Over the Top!

To create her finely textured, deeply embossed artwork, artist Evelyn Rosenberg of Albuquerque, New Mexico, makes use of . . .

a. plastic explosives.
b. hand grenades.
c. fireworks.
d. huge bonfires.

#3 It's a Wrap

Whether it's wrapping entire buildings, surrounding islands with pink fabric, or wrapping 178 trees with translucent material, artists Christo and Jeanne-Claude use the whole world as a canvas for their art.

#2 Made to Scale

Harold Dalton, a 19th-century American artist, created works of art using the scales from butterfly wings. After removing the scales, he sorted them by color. Then he puffed air through a small glass tube to position each scale on a glass slide and crushed it to release the oil that would hold it in place. The completed masterpieces were no bigger than a postage stamp.

#1 Beetlemania

Artist Jan Fabre was hired by the Queen of Belgium to redecorate the Hall of Mirrors in the Royal Palace in Brussels. To the queen's astonishment, Fabre used the shiny, iridescent wing cases of Asian jewel beetles to create a mural as well as to cover the main chandelier.

Many of the things that have been and are still being done in the name of beauty are truly unbelievable. Three of the facts below are true. Can you pick out the one that's as fake as false eyelashes?

a. In China, up until the early 20th century, many three-year-old girls had their toes broken and their feet tightly bound with cloth to keep them from growing more than four inches long. Otherwise, they might not have attracted husbands.

Believe It!   **Not!**

b. In the 1990s, Elizabeth Christensen spent 250,000 dollars on 240 operations to sculpt her face into a likeness of Nefertiti, an ancient Egyptian queen noted for her beauty.

Believe It!   **Not!**

c. The ancient Maya people frequently sharpened their teeth to a fine point and inserted jewels into them.

Believe It!   **Not!**

d. To achieve the full-lipped look that is all the rage today, many young women who can't afford collagen treatments coat their lips with honey to attract bees in the hope of being stung so their lips will swell up.

Believe It!   **Not!**

BONUS QUESTION

Each year, in the belief that it will assure the speedy recovery of sick relatives, more than 5,000 people in India . . .

a. eat nothing but bread and water for three months.

b. walk through flames.

c. shave their heads.

d. wear sackcloth and ashes for six months.

POP QUIZ

Are you all topped out? Of course you're not!
Now it's time for you to test your knowledge of the
weirdest of the weird and see just how well you
remember some of the incredible facts in *Top 10!*

1. The Mangbetu people of Central Africa consider it a
sign of great beauty if you have . . .
a. enlarged lips.
b. gold teeth.
c. a long neck.
d. an elongated head.

2. The skill of distorting one's features into weird-
looking faces is called . . .
a. girning.
b. elasting.
c. plasticizing.
d. rubber-necking.

3. The 2003 Bug Bowl held at Rutgers University
introduced a new game called . . .
a. snail racing.
b. cockroach scramble.
c. cricket spitting.
d. butterfly flutters.

4. At the Thai Elephant Conservation Center, elephants have been trained to . . .

a. paint watercolors.

b. play in an orchestra.

c. stand on their heads.

d. ballet dance.

5. George, a schnauzer trained by Duane Pickel, can . . .

a. sniff out cancer before it becomes a threat.

b. understand 200 words spoken in German.

c. water-ski.

d. do tricks on a skateboard.

6. After she had a heart attack, Jo Altsman's life was saved when help was attracted by her pet . . .

a. miniature horse.

b. parrot.

c. potbellied pig.

d. chimpanzee.

7. In 2000, street magician David Blaine spent 62 hours inside a six-ton block of ice.

Believe It!   **Not!**

8. In the 1990s, a popular restaurant in Washington, D.C., was called . . .

a. The Elephant's Trunk.

b. The Porkbarrel.

c. The Donkey's Ears.

d. The Insect Club.

9. The drops of moisture released when you sneeze travel at speeds up to . . .

a. 31 miles per hour.

b. 76 miles per hour.

c. 102 miles per hour.

d. 184 miles per hour.

10. After she died, Edna MacArthur's body was cremated and her ashes were . . .

a. put into an Etch-A-Sketch.

b. turned into a diamond ring.

c. incorporated in an artificial reef.

d. made into bone china.

11. German professor Gunther von Hagens turns donated human corpses into works of art.

Believe It!   **Not!**

12. At Captain Joseph Belain's burial service, . . .

a. his parrot perched on his coffin and sang "Row, Row, Row Your Boat."

b. a carrier pigeon perched on the bier and stayed until the service ended.

c. an eagle dropped a large fish on his coffin.

d. his black cat sat on the coffin and howled.

13. At the annual Naadam Festival in Mongolia, children ages four to twelve . . .

a. ride in an 18-mile-long horse race.

b. compete in a camel-jumping contest.

c. dance nonstop for 12 hours.

d. vie to see who can build the best sandcastle.

14. A chapel on the Isle of Guernsey in Great Britain is made entirely of human bones.

Believe It!   **Not!**

15. Harry Dalton was a 19th-century artist who created detailed works of art using only . . .

a. seaweed

b. pigeon feathers.

c. the scales from butterfly wings.

d. the wing cases of Asian jewel beetles.

Answer Key

Chapter 1
Odd Folk

Page 5:   **d.** had her lower ribs surgically removed.
Page 7:   **b.** blacken their teeth.
Page 9:   **d.** two left hands.
Page 11:   **d.** three tongues.
Page 13:   **a.** submerged up to his neck in the ocean.
Page 15:   **b.** form the letters of the alphabet.
Brain Buster: c. is false.
Bonus Question: d.

Chapter 2
Critters

Page 19:   **b.** riding a skateboard.
Page 21:   **d.** multiply, divide, and do square roots.
Page 23:   **a.** Revheim is about to have an epileptic
            seizure.
Page 24:   **b.** Drew Barrymore
Page 27:   **d.** two-headed king snake.
Page 29:   **c.** swan-shaped boat.
Brain Buster: b. is false.
Bonus Question: d.

Chapter 3
That's X-treme

Page 33: **d.** hanging by her mouth from a bar attached to the rope.

Page 35: **a.** wearing a full suit of armor and dragging a 38-pound weight.

Page 37: **b.** it is banned from many hotels and buses.

Page 39: **a.** a horde of snails slimed the tracks.

Page 41: **c.** put a live frog in his or her mouth.

Page 43: **d.** boiled Egyptian mummy skin and wrappings.

Brain Buster: a. is false.

Bonus Question: a.

Chapter 4
Creepy!

Page 47: **a.** is a table on which a daily meal is served for his soul.

Page 49: **d.** hoisted onto the shoulders of the village blacksmith, who dances with it for hours.

Page 51 **a.** The groom was a corpse.

Page 53: **b.** kept his embalmed head in a bag for the last 29 years of her life.

Page 55: **a.** roots of the tree slowly absorbed his body and assumed a human shape.

Page 57: **c.** Nero took his own life in a villa four miles away.

Brain Buster: d. is false.

Bonus Question: c.

Chapter 5
Totally Weird

Page 61: **a.** spray colored water all over each other.

Page 63: **d.** drink a cup of wine containing a live goldfish.

Page 65: **b.** entirely underground.

Page 66: **d.** 900 bags of musk so that it would always smell like perfume.

Page 69: **b.** toilet paper.

Page 71: **a.** plastic explosives.

Brain Buster: d. is false.

Bonus Question: b.

Pop Quiz

1. **d.**
2. **a.**
3. **c.**
4. **b.**
5. **a.**
6. **c.**
7. **Believe It!**
8. **d.**
9. **c.**
10. **b.**
11. **Believe It!**
12. **b.**
13. **a.**
14. **Not!**
15. **c.**

What's Your Ripley's Rank?

Ripley's Scorecard

Congratulations! You've busted your brain over some of the weirdest behavior in the world and proven your ability to tell fact from fiction. Now it's time to rate your Ripley's knowledge. Are you a **Nonstarter** or a **Top Banana**? Check out the answer key and use this page to keep track of how many trivia questions you answered correctly. Then tally them up and find out how you rate.

Here's the scoring breakdown. Give yourself:
★ **10 points** for every **Over the Top!** you answered correctly;
★ **20 points** for every fiction you spotted in the **Ripley's Brain Busters**;
★ **10 points** every time you answered a **Bonus Question**;
★ and **5 points** for every **Pop Quiz** question you answered right.

Here's a tally sheet:

Number of **Over the Top!**
questions answered correctly: _____ x 10 = _____

Number of **Ripley's Brain Buster**
fictions spotted: _____ x 20 = _____

Number of **Bonus Questions**
answered correctly: _____ x 10 = _____

Number of **Pop Quiz** questions
answered correctly: _____ x 5 = _____

Total the right column for your final score: _____

0–100
Nonstarter

Okay, so maybe you're not that interested in Top 10 lists. Or maybe you just don't like the categories we chose—or have your own ideas about what should be included on the Top 10 in each one. No problem. There are lots more Ripley's Believe It or Not! books to check out. *Weird Pet Stories* is perfect if you're an animal lover. If you're the adventuresome type, try *X-traordinary X-tremes*. If you're a scholar, however, *Strange School Stories* is just the book you're looking for.

101–250
Inching Up

You've made a good start, so it's clear you enjoy reading about the weirdest and wackiest facts in the Ripley archives. You still need some practice at separating fact from fiction, but you're definitely beginning to inch your way up the list of Ripley experts.

251–400
Almost There

Wow! It looks like Top 10 lists of really weird facts are right up your alley! You've proven that you have a knack for soaking up astonishing facts—and remembering them, to boot. Keep going, and it won't be long before you make it to the top of the Ripley expert list!

401–575
Top Banana
Congratulations! Not only have you proven that you're an ace at separating truly weird facts from weird but totally bogus facts, you've also shown that your knowledge and interests are wide-ranging. Now that you've made it to the top of the list of Ripley experts, there'll be no stopping you!

Believe It!®

Photo Credits

Ripley Entertainment Inc. and the editors of this book wish to thank the following photographers, agents, and other individuals for permission to use and reprint the following photographs in this book. Any photographs included in this book that are not acknowledged below are property of the Ripley Archives. Great effort has been made to obtain permission from the owners of all materials included in this book. Any errors that may have been made are unintentional and will gladly be corrected in future printings if notice is sent to Ripley Entertainment Inc., 7576 Kingspointe Parkway, Suite #188, Orlando, Florida 32819.

Black & White Photos

8 Tom Leppard/MURDOPHOTO.COM

16 Robert John Burck/© J. W. Richards

20 Ron Sirull and Brutus/Aerialfocus.com/ Tom Anders

23 Dan Shaw and Cuddles/Courtesy Janet Burleson

25 Kangaroo/Ablestock

26 Troy Sica and Bullet/Alejandra Villa/ © 2004 Newsday/Reprinted with Permission

27 Snail/Getty Images/Brand X Pictures

28 Prince Charming/Henry Lizardlover

33 Sebastien Foucan/Jamie Fry/EPA Photo/AP

40 Caterpillar with Wasp Larvae/© Corel Images

41 Sneeze/© Lester V. Bergman/CORBIS

42 Alexis St. Martin and William Beaumont/ LC-USZCN4-70/Library of Congress Prints & Photographs Division

44 X-ray/Ygal Levi/Reuters Pictures Archive/Newscom

48 Fireworks/Ablestock

52 Si Quey/Courtesy of Alf Erickson

56 Mary Todd Lincoln/The Lincoln Museum/Fort Wayne, IN (#109)

58 Staircase/Courtesy Winchester Mystery House, San Jose, CA

63 Wodaabe Beauty Contest/© Tiziana and Gianni Baldizzone/CORBIS

64 Land Diver/Patrick Krohn

67 National Fresh Water Fishing Hall of Fame/Courtesy National Fresh Water Fishing Hall of Fame

68 Lucy/Photograph Courtesy of the Save Lucy Committee/www.lucytheelephant.org

70 Guitar Motorcycle/Guitcycle © Ray Nelson/www.guitarsnotguns.org/Photo © Harrod Blank/www.artcaragency.com

72 Jan Fabre Chandelier/Dirk Pauwels

Color Insert

Plastinized Corpse/Wiggles Kirsty Wigglesworth/PA Photos/Newscom

Extreme Ironing/PR Newswire/Newscom;

Vegetarian Festival/STR/Reuters Pictures Archive

Dani Mummy/Rosanne Pennella/ www.rosannepennella.com

Karni Mata Temple/Kamal Kishore/Reuters Pictures Archive

Elaine Davidson/Mark Campbell/ www.silentsongs.co.uk

Norman Gary/Rich Pedroncelli/AP

Cover

Dog/Courtesy of dog-goes GmbH; Image the Kitten/AP Photo/*Courier Times*/Jay Crawford

Don't miss these  other exciting books . . .

World's Weirdest
Critters

Creepy Stuff

Odd-inary
People

Amazing
Escapes

World's Weirdest
Gadgets

Bizarre Bugs

Blasts from
the Past

Awesome
Animals

Weird
Science

X-traordinary
X-tremes

Strange School
Stories

Weird Pet
Stories

WE'D LOVE TO BELIEVE
YOU!

Do you have a Believe It or Not!
story that has happened to you or to someone
you know? If it's weird enough and if you would
like to share it, the people at Ripley's would love
to hear about it. You can send your
Believe It or Not! entries to:

**The Director of the Archives
Ripley Entertainment Inc.
7576 Kingspointe Parkway,
Suite 188
Orlando, Florida 32819**

Believe It!®